THE CREATION OF THE WORLD

Basil

Copyright © 2014 Beloved Publishing

All rights reserved. No part of this book may be reproduced, scanned, or distributed in any printed or electronic form without permission.

Printed in the United States of America

ISBN:1631740865

BIOGRAPHICAL NOTE

Basil, bishop of Caesarea in Cappadocia, and styled "The Great," was the founder of Eastern monasticism, defender of the Nicene doctrines and doctor of the Church. He was born at Caesarea in 329, and was thoroughly educated in all that a teacher like Libanius could impart at Rome, and Himerius at Constantinople. Returning home, he plunged into the pleasures of social life, but was induced by his sister to visit the hermits of Syria, Palestine and Egypt. Attracted during his travels to the religious life, he secluded himself in a lonely spot in inclement Pontus.

During his monastic life of seven years (357-364) he formulated the monastic rule still observed by Eastern monks. Ordained presbyter in 364, he labored in founding religious institutions of various kinds. He attracted notice by his growing Nicene predilections, and was elected bishop of his native town (370) and virtual primate of Asia Minor. His conduct in dealing with the Arians was uncompromising yet conciliating. As a theologian he stands next to his brother Gregory and to Athanasius, but he excels them both in the literary charm and variety of his Greek style. He died in 379.

BASIL 329-379

THE CREATION OF THE WORLD

The earth was without form and void.—Gen. i, 2.

In the few words which have occupied us this morning we have found such a depth of thought that we despair of penetrating farther. If such is the forecourt of the sanctuary, if the portico of the temple is so grand and magnificent, if the splendor of its beauty thus dazzles the eyes of the soul, what will be the holy of holies? Who will dare to try to gain access to the innermost shrine? Who will look into its secrets? To gaze into it is indeed forbidden us, and language is powerless to express what the mind conceives.

However, since there are rewards, and most desirable ones, reserved by the just Judge for the intention alone of doing good, do not let us hesitate to continue our researches. Altho we may not attain to the truth, if, with the help of the Spirit, we do not fall away from the meaning of Holy Scripture, we shall not deserve to be rejected, and with the help of grace, we shall contribute to the edification of the Church of God.

"The earth," says Holy Scripture, "was without form and void"—*i.e.*, invisible and unfinished. The heavens and the earth were created together. How, then, is it that the heavens are perfect whilst the earth is still unformed and incomplete? In one word, what was the unfinished condition of the earth and for what reason was it invisible? The fertility of the earth is its perfect finishing; growth of all kinds of plants, the up-springing of tall trees, both productive and unfruitful, flowers' sweet scents and fair colors, and all that which, a little later, at the voice of God came forth from the earth to beautify her, their universal mother.

As nothing of all this yet existed, Scripture is right in calling the earth "without form." We could also say of the heavens that they were still imperfect and had not received their natural adornment, since at that time they did not shine with the glory of the sun and of the moon, and were not crowned by the choirs of the stars. These bodies were not yet created. Thus you will not diverge from the truth in saying that the heavens also were "without form." The earth was invisible for two reasons: it may be because man, the spectator, did not yet exist, or because, being submerged under the waters which overflowed the surface, it could not be seen, since the waters had not yet been gathered together into their own places, where God afterward collected them and gave them the name of sea.

What is invisible? First of all, that which our fleshly eye can not perceive—our mind, for example; then that which, visible in its nature, is hidden by some body which conceals it, like iron in the depths of the earth. It is in this sense that the earth, in that it was hidden under the waters, was still invisible. However, as light did not yet exist, and as the earth lay in darkness because of the obscurity of the air above it, it should not astonish us that for this reason Scripture calls it "invisible."

But the corrupters of the truth, who, incapable of submitting their reason to Holy Scripture, distort at will the meaning of the Holy Scriptures, pretend that these words mean matter. For it is matter, they say, which from its nature is without form and invisible—being by the conditions of its existence without quality and without form and figure. The Artificer submitting it to the working of His wisdom clothed it with a form, organized it, and thus gave being to the visible world.

If the matter is uncreated, it has a claim to the same honors as God, since it must be of equal rank with Him. Is this not the summit of wickedness that utter chaos, without quality, without form or shape, ugliness without configuration, to use their own expression, should enjoy the same prerogatives as He who is wisdom, power, and beauty itself, the Creator and the Demiurge of the universe enjoys? This is not all. If the matter is so great as to be capable of being acted on by the whole wisdom of God, it would in a way raise its hypostasis to an equality with the inaccessible power of God, since it would be able to measure by itself all the extent of the divine intelligence.

If it is insufficient for the operations of God, then we fall into a more absurd blasphemy, since we condemn God for not being able, on account of the want of matter, to finish His own works. The resourcelessness of human nature has deceived these reasoners. Each of our crafts is exercised upon some special matter—the art of the smith upon iron, that of the carpenter on wood. In all there is the subject, the form and the work which results from the form. Matter is taken from without —art gives the form—and the work is composed at the same time of form and of matter.

Such is the idea that they make for themselves of the divine work. The form of the world is due to the wisdom of the supreme Artificer; matter came to the Creator from without; and thus the world results from a double origin. It has received from outside its matter and its essence, and from God its form and figure. They thus come to deny that the mighty God has presided at the formation of the universe, and pretend that he has only brought a crowning contribution to a common work; that he has only contributed some small portion to the genesis of beings; they are incapable, from the debasement of their reasonings, of raising their glances to the height of truth. Here, below, arts are subsequent to matter—introduced into life by the indispensable need of them. Wool existed before weaving made it supply one of nature's imperfections. Wood existed before carpentering took possession of it, and transformed it each day to supply new wants and made us see all the advantages derived from it, giving the oar to the sailor, the winnowing-fan to the laborer, the lance to the soldier.

But God, before all those things which now attract our notice existed, after casting about in His mind and determining to bring into being that which had no being, imagined the world such as it ought to be, and created matter in harmony with the form which He wished to give it. He assigned to the heavens the nature adapted for the heavens, and gave to the earth an essence in accordance with its form. He formed, as he wished, fire, air, and water, and gave to each the essence which the object of its existence required.

Finally he welded all the diverse parts of the universe by links of indissoluble attachment and established between them so perfect a fellowship and harmony that the most distant, in spite of their distance, appeared united in one universal sympathy. Let those men, therefore, renounce their fabulous imaginations, who in spite of the weakness of their argument, pretend to measure a power as incomprehensible to man's reason as it is unutterable by man's voice.

God created the heavens and the earth, but not only one-half of each; He created all the heavens and all the earth, creating the essence with the form. For He is not an inventor of figures, but the Creator even of the essence of beings. Further, let them tell us how the efficient power of God could deal with the passive nature of matter, the latter furnishing the matter without form, the former possessing the science of the form without matter, both being in need of each other; the Creator in order to display his art, matter in order to cease to be without form and to receive a form. But let us stop here and return to our subject.

"The earth was invisible and unfinished." In saying "In the beginning God created the heavens and the earth" the sacred writer passed over many things in silence—water, air, fire, and the results from them, which, all forming in reality the true complement of the world, were, without doubt made at the same time as the universe. By this silence history wishes to train the activity of our intelligence, giving it a weak point for starting, to impel it to the discovery of the truth.

Thus, we are told of the creation of water; but, as we are told that the earth was invisible, ask yourself what could have covered it and prevented it from being seen? Fire could not conceal it. Fire brightens all about it, and spreads light rather than darkness around. No more was it air that enveloped the earth. Air by nature is of little density and transparent. It receives all kinds of visible objects and transmits them to the spectators. Only one supposition remains: that which floated on the surface of the earth was water, the fluid essence which had not yet been confined to its own place.

Thus the earth was not only invisible; it was still incomplete. Even to-day excessive damp is a hindrance to the productiveness of the earth. The same cause at the same time prevents it from being seen and from being complete, for the proper and natural adornment of the earth is its completion: corn waving in the valleys, meadows green with grass and rich with many-colored flowers, fertile glades and hilltops shaded by forests. Of all this nothing was yet produced; the earth was in travail with it in virtue of the power that she had received from the Creator. But she was waiting for the appointed time and the divine order to bring forth.

"Darkness was upon the face of the deep." A new source for fables and most impious imaginations may be found by distorting the sense of these words at the will of one's fancies. By "darkness" these wicked men do not understand what is meant in reality—air not illumined, the shadow produced by the interposition of a body, or finally a place for some reason deprived of light. For them "darkness" is an evil power, or rather the personification of evil, having his origin in himself in opposition to, and in perpetual struggle with, the goodness of God. If God is light, they say, without any doubt the power which struggles against Him must be darkness, "darkness" not owing its existence to a foreign origin, but an evil existing by itself. "Darkness" is the enemy of souls, the primary cause of death, the adversary of virtue. The words of the prophet, they say in their error, show that it exists and that it does not proceed from God. From this what perverse and impious dogmas have been imagined! What grievous wolves, tearing the flock of the Lord, have sprung from these words to cast themselves upon souls! Is it not from hence that have come forth Marcions and Valentinuses and the detestable heresy of the Manicheans which you may, without going far wrong, call the putrid humor of the churches?

O man, why wander thus from the truth and imagine for thyself that which will cause thy perdition? The word is simple and within the comprehension of all. "The earth was invisible." Why? Because the "deep" was spread over its surface. What is "the deep?" A mass of water of extreme depth. But we know that we can see many bodies through clear and transparent water. How, then, was it that no part of the earth appeared through the water? Because the air which surrounded it was still without light and in darkness. The rays of the sun, penetrating the water, often allow us to see the pebbles which form the bed of the river, but in a dark night it is impossible for our glance to penetrate under the water. Thus, these words, "the earth was invisible," are explained by those that follow; "the deep" covered it and itself was in darkness. Thus the deep is not a multitude of hostile powers, as has been imagined; nor "darkness" an evil sovereign force in enmity with good. In reality two rival principles of equal power, if engaged without ceasing in a war of mutual attacks, will end in self-destruction.

But if one should gain the mastery it would completely annihilate the conquered. Thus, to maintain the balance in the struggle between good and evil is to represent them as engaged in a war without end and in perpetual destruction, where the opponents are at the same time conquerors and conquered. If good is the stronger, what is there to prevent evil from being completely annihilated? But if that be the case, the very utterance of which is impious, I ask myself how it is that they themselves are not filled with horror to think that they have imagined such abominable blasphemies.

It is equally impious to say that evil has its origin from God; because the contrary can not proceed from its contrary. Life does not engender death; darkness is not the origin of light; sickness is not the maker of health. In the changes of conditions there are transitions from one condition to the contrary; but in genesis each being proceeds from its like and from its contrary. If, then, evil is neither uncreated nor created by God, from whence comes its nature? Certainly, that evil exists no one living in the world will deny. What shall we say, then? Evil is not a living animated essence: it is the condition of the soul opposed to virtue, developed in the careless on account of their falling away from good.

Do not, then, go beyond yourself to seek for evil, and imagine that there is an original nature of wickedness. Each of us—let us acknowledge it—is the first author of his own vice.

Among the ordinary events of life, some come naturally, like old age and sickness; others by chance, like unforeseen occurrences, of which the origin is beyond ourselves, often sad, sometimes fortunate—as, for instance, the discovery of a treasure when digging a well, or the meeting of a mad dog when going to the market-place.

Others depend upon ourselves; such as ruling one's passions, or not putting a bridle on one's pleasures; the mastery of anger, or resistance against him who irritates us; truth-telling or lying, the maintenance of a sweet and well-regulated disposition, or of a mood fierce and swollen and exalted with pride. Here you are the master of your actions. Do not look for the guiding cause beyond yourself, but recognize that evil, rightly so called, has no other origin than our voluntary falls. If it were involuntary, and did not depend upon ourselves, the laws would not have so much terror for the guilty, and the tribunals would not be so pitiless when they condemn wretches according to the measure of their crimes.

But enough concerning evil rightly so called. Sickness, poverty, obscurity, death, finally all human afflictions, ought not to be ranked as evils, since we do not count among the greatest boons things which are their opposites. Among these afflictions some are the effect of nature, others have obviously been for many a source of advantage. Let us be silent for the moment about these metaphors and allegories, and, simply following without vain curiosity the words of Holy Scripture, let us take from darkness the idea which it gives us.

But reason asks, Was darkness created with the world? Is it older than light? Why, in spite of its inferiority, has it preceded it? Darkness, we reply, did not exist in essence; it is a condition produced in the air by the withdrawal of light. What, then, is that light which disappeared suddenly from the world so that darkness should cover the face of the deep? If anything had existed before the formation of this sensible and perishable world, no doubt we conclude it would have been in the light. The orders of angels, the heavenly hosts, all intellectual natures named or unnamed, all the ministering spirits, did not live in darkness, but enjoyed a condition fitted for them in light and spiritual joy.

No one will contradict this, least of all he who looks for celestial light as one of the rewards promised to virtue—the light which, as Solomon says, is always a light to the righteous, the light which made the apostle say, "Giving thanks unto the Father, which hath made us meet to be partakers of the inheritance of the saints in light." Finally, if the condemned are sent into outer darkness, evidently those who are made worthy of God's approval are at rest in heavenly light. When, then, according to the order of God, the heaven appeared, enveloping all that its circumference included, a vast and unbroken body separating outer things from those which it enclosed, it necessarily kept the space inside in darkness for want of communication with the outer light.

Three things are, indeed, needed to form a shadow: light, a body, a dark place. The shadow of heaven forms the darkness of the world. Understand, I pray you, what I mean, by a simple example—by raising for yourself at midday a tent of some compact and impenetrable material, you shut yourself up in sudden darkness. Suppose that original darkness was like this, not subsisting directly by itself, but resulting from some external causes. If it is said that it rested upon the deep, it is because the extremity of air naturally touches the surface of bodies; and as at that time the water covered everything, we are obliged to say that darkness was upon the face of the deep.

"And the Spirit of God moved upon the face of the waters?" Does this Spirit mean the diffusion of air? The sacred writer wishes to enumerate to you the elements of the world, to tell you that God created the heavens, the earth, water and air, and that the last was now diffused and in motion; or rather, that which is truer and confirmed by the authority of the ancients, by the Spirit of God he means the Holy Spirit. It is, as has been remarked, the special name, the name above all others that Scripture delights to give to the Holy Spirit, and by the Spirit of God the Holy Spirit is meant, the Spirit, namely, which completes the divine and blessed Trinity. You will always find it better, therefore, to take it in this sense. How, then, did the Spirit of God move upon the waters? The explanation that I am about to give you is not an original one, but that of a Syrian who was as ignorant in the wisdom of this world as he was versed in the knowledge of the truth.

He said, then, that the Syriac word was more expressive, and that, being more analogous to the Hebrew term, it was a nearer approach to the Scriptural sense. This is the meaning of the word: by "moved" the Syrians, he says, understand brooded over. The Spirit cherished the nature of the waters as one sees a bird cover the eggs with her body and impart to them vital force from her own warmth. Such is, as nearly as possible, the meaning of these words—the Spirit moved: that is, prepared the nature of water to produce living beings: a sufficient proof for those who ask if the Holy Spirit took an active part in the creation of the world.

"And God said, Let there be light." The first word uttered by God created the nature of light; it made darkness vanish, dispelled gloom, illuminated the world, and gave to all being at the same time a sweet and gracious aspect. The heavens, until then enveloped in darkness, appeared with that beauty which they still present to our eyes. The air was lighted up, or rather made the light circulate mixed with its substance, and, distributing its splendor rapidly in every direction, so dispersed itself to its extreme limits. Up it sprang to the very ether and heaven. In an instant it lighted up the whole extent of the world, the north and the south, the east and the west. For the ether also is such a subtle substance and so transparent that it needs not the space of a moment for light to pass through it. Just as it carries our sight instantaneously to the object of vision, so without the least interval, with a rapidity that thought can not conceive, it receives these rays of light in its uttermost limits. With light the ether becomes more pleasing and the waters more limpid. These last, not content with receiving its splendor, return it by the reflection of light and in all directions send forth quivering flashes. The divine word gives every object a more cheerful and a more attractive appearance, just as when men pour in oil into the deep sea they make the place about them smooth. So, with a single word and in one instant the Creator of all things gave the boon of light to the world.

"Let there be light." The order was itself an operation, and a state of things was brought into being than which man's mind can not even imagine a pleasanter one for our enjoyment It must be well understood that when we speak of the voice, of the word, of the command of God, this divine language does not mean to us a sound which escapes from the organs of speech, a collision of air struck by the tongue; it is a simple sign of the will of God, and, if we give it the form of an order, it is only the better to impress the souls whom we instruct.

"And God saw the light, that it was good." How can we worthily praise light after the testimony given by the Creator to its goodness? The word, even among us, refers the judgment to the eyes, incapable of raising itself to the idea that the senses have already received. But if beauty in bodies results from symmetry of parts and the harmonious appearance of colors how, in a simple and homogeneous essence like light, can this idea of beauty be preserved? Would not the symmetry in light be less shown in its parts than in the pleasure and delight at the sight of it? Such is also the beauty of gold, which it owes, not to the happy mingling of its parts, but only to its beautiful color, which has a charm attractive to the eyes.

Thus, again, the evening star is the most beautiful of the stars: not that the parts of which it is composed form a harmonious whole, but thanks to the unalloyed and beautiful brightness which meets our eyes. And further, when God proclaimed the goodness of light, it was not in regard to the charm of the eye, but as a provision for future advantage, because at that time there were as yet no eyes to judge of its beauty.

"And God divided the light from the darkness." That is to say, God gave them natures incapable of mixing, perpetually in opposition to each other, and put between them the widest space and distance.

"And God called the light day, and the darkness he called night." Since the birth of the sun, the light that it diffuses in the air when shining on our hemisphere is day, and the shadow produced by its disappearance is night. But at that time it was not after the movement of the sun, but following this primitive light spread abroad in the air or withdrawn in a measure determined by God, that day came and was followed by night.

"And the evening and the morning were the first day." Evening is then the boundary common to day and night; and in the same way morning constitutes the approach of night to day. It was to give day the privileges of seniority that Scripture put the end of the first day before that of the first night, because night follows day: for, before the creation of light, the world was not in night, but in darkness. It is the opposite of day which was called night, and it did not receive its name until after day. Thus were created the evening and the morning. Scripture means the space of a day and a night, and afterward no more says day and night, but calls them both under the name of the more important: a custom which you will find throughout Scripture. Everywhere the measure of time is counted by days without mention of nights. "The days of our years," says the Psalmist; "few and evil have the days of the years of my life been," said Jacob; and elsewhere "all the days of my life."

"And the evening and the morning were the first day," or, rather, one day.—(*Revised Vers*). Why does Scripture say "one day," not "the first day?" Before speaking to us of the second, the third, and the fourth days, would it not have been more natural to call that one the first which began the series? If it, therefore, says "one day," it is from a wish to determine the measure of day and night and to combine the time that they contain. Now, twenty-four hours fill up the space of one day—we mean of a day and of a night; and if, at the time of the solstices, they have not both an equal length, the time marked by Scripture does not the less circumscribe their duration. It is as tho it said: Twenty-four hours measure the space of a day, or a day is in reality the time that the heavens, starting from one point, take to return thither. Thus, every time that, in the revolution of the sun, evening and morning occupy the world, their periodical succession never exceeds the space of one day.

But we must believe that there is a mysterious reason for this? God, who made the nature of time, measured it out and determined it by intervals of days; and, wishing to give it a week as a measure, he ordered the week to resolve from period to period upon itself, to count the movement of time, forming the week of one day revolving seven times upon itself: a proper circle begins and ends with itself. Such is also the character of eternity, to revolve upon itself and to end nowhere. If, then, the beginning of time is called "one day" rather than "the first day," it is because Scripture wishes to establish its relationship with eternity. It was, in reality, fit and natural to call "one" the day whose character is to be one wholly separated and isolated from all others. If Scripture speaks to us of many ages, saying everywhere "age of age, and ages of ages," we do not see it enumerate them as first, second, and third. It follows that we are hereby shown, not so much limits, ends, and succession of ages as distinctions between various states and modes of action. "The day of the Lord," Scripture says, "is great and very terrible," and elsewhere, "Woe unto you that desire the day of the Lord: to what end is it for you? The day of the Lord is darkness and not light." A day of darkness for those who are worthy of darkness. No; this day without evening, without succession, and without end is not unknown to Scripture, and it is the day that the Psalmist calls the eighth day, because it is outside this time of weeks. Thus, whether you call it day or whether you call it eternity, you express the same idea. Give this state the name of day; there are not several, but only one. If you call it eternity still it is unique and not manifold. Thus it is in order that you may carry your thoughts forward toward a future life that Scripture marks by the word "one" the day which is the type of eternity, the first-fruits of days, the contemporary of light, the holy Lord's day.

But while I am conversing with you about the first evening of the world, evening takes me by surprize and puts an end to my discourse. May the Father of the true light, who has adorned day with celestial light, who has made to shine the fires which illuminate us during the night, who reserves for us in the peace of a future age a spiritual and everlasting light, enlighten your hearts in the knowledge of truth, keep you from stumbling, and grant that "you may walk honestly as in the day." Thus shall you shine as the sun in the midst of the glory of the saints, and I shall glory in you in the day of Christ, to whom belong all glory and power for ever and ever. Amen.

Made in the USA
Columbia, SC
25 May 2025